FIRST AID FOR

broken
hearts

FIRST AID FOR
broken hearts

ALAN D. WOLFELT, PH.D.

Companion Press is an imprint of the Center for Loss and Life Transition, 3735 Broken Bow Road, Fort Collins, Colorado 80526.

Companion Press books may be purchased in bulk for sales promotions, premiums, and fundraisers. Please contact the publisher at the above address for more information.

25 24 23   6 5 4 3

ISBN: 978-1-61722-281-8

In memory of my parents,
Donald and Virgene Wolfelt,
who inspired me to live a
life of service to others.

contents

introduction

"HEALING TAKES COURAGE,
AND WE ALL HAVE COURAGE,
EVEN IF WE HAVE TO DIG
A LITTLE TO FIND IT."

— TORI AMOS

we meet here,
on this page,
because your
heart is broken.

You're hurting. You're suffering life's most painful experience: loss.

Whatever your loss may be, please know that I am genuinely sorry.

I've been a grief counselor and educator for a long time now. Doing what I can to offer compassion and hope to people who are grieving is my passion and life's work.

As you well know, your grief is real. I hope this book helps you in two important ways:

1. **to honor your unique grief, and**

2. **to help you mend your heart.**

Does mending seem impossible to you right now? If so, that's OK. You are where you are.

Yet I assure you that not only is mending possible, it can transform you. We'll step through it together.

Welcome to *First Aid for Broken Hearts.*

Brokenheartedness

Life is both wonderful and devastating.

It graces us with joy, and it breaks our hearts.

Why are our hearts so breakable? Because human hearts are made to grow attached.

IF WE'RE LUCKY, THAT IS.

If we're lucky, we love. If we're fortunate, we become attached.

Our loves and attachments are what give our fleeting, challenging lives meaning and joy.

But—and this may be the biggest Catch-22 in all of human existence!—there's an unavoidable flipside to the joy of connection: Whenever our loves and attachments are threatened, torn, or broken, our hearts begin to break.

When we love someone and they die, our hearts break.

When we love someone and we become separated from them, our hearts break.

When we love someone and they get seriously sick, our hearts break.

When we are powerfully attached to a place or a home, a career or a situation, that we must transition away from, our hearts break.

In the course of our decades of life, that's an awful lot of brokenheartedness for each of us to bear.

DEGREES OF BROKENNESS

How badly our hearts break each time we lose something is generally a measure of two things: the strength of the attachment bond, and the severity of the threat to the bond.

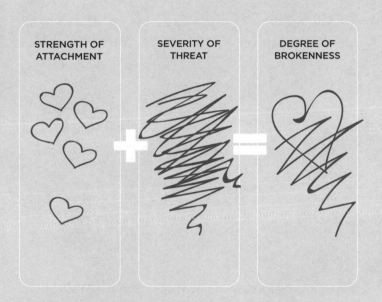

| STRENGTH OF ATTACHMENT | | SEVERITY OF THREAT | | DEGREE OF BROKENNESS |

Of course, brokenheartedness can't actually be quantified. As with all emotional and spiritual experiences, there is no objective unit of measure. We can't weigh it on a scale or wrap it with a measuring tape.

Yet even though we can't assign our brokenheartedness a precise number, we instinctively know how broken we feel inside. Those of us who've been on this earth for a while know that sometimes our hearts sustain more damage than at other times.

| Some losses hurt just a twinge. | Some losses are painful but manageable. | And some losses knock us to the ground and rip our hearts from our chests. |

If your loss was especially damaging and perhaps recent, you may even be wondering if you'll survive. As my friend and colleague Earl Grollman once said, "The worst grief is the one you are going through right now."

Yet no matter how badly broken your heart is at this moment, the principles in this book will help you mend. That is my promise.

life is change

Love and attachment are indeed wonderful, but the circumstances of life are impermanent.

No matter how devotedly we love and try to safeguard our attachments, the globe spins. The years pass. And things change.

People get sick.

People age.

People die.

Pets too.

People betray us.

We betray ourselves.

Passions ebb and flow.

Fortunes rise and fall.

And no matter what happens, the world just keeps turning.

Life is like a river.
We are floating down a
river that twists and turns.
We can never see very far ahead.
Sometimes the going is smooth;
sometimes the rapids are rocky
and dangerous. And sometimes
a waterfall plunges us over the edge.

Life is constant change, which means the circumstances in which we love and are attached are also constantly changing. No matter how hard we try to manage risk and control our destinies, things inevitably happen that turn our lives upside-down.

ANYTIME WE GAIN SOMETHING NEW, WE GIVE SOMETHING ELSE UP.

Sometimes we choose the things or people to give up. Other times they're torn away from us against our will. Either way, we're bound to suffer loss.

The longer we live, the more the losses pile up. It's unavoidable. Unless we don't love or grow attached at all, of course. But what kind of life would that be?

death. job loss. broken dreams. estrangement. abuse. betrayal. separation. illness. divorce.

Heartbreakers

Human hearts break for many reasons. All are real, valid, and painful.

Death of a loved one

Divorce

Break-ups

Illness (yourself or someone you care about)

Emotional estrangement from a loved one

Physical separation from a loved one

Loss of a pet

"Burst bubbles" (realizations that cherished people or things were not what you believed, hoped, or dreamed them to be)

Betrayals

Abuse

Lost or broken dreams

Traumatic accidents or events

Leaving a home

Financial losses

Job change or loss

This isn't an exhaustive list, of course. Whatever has broken your heart, it also belongs on this page.

My own heart has been broken many times in my life, by the deaths of beloved people, by significant relationships ending, by health crises, and by my family's house burning down.

So tell me, what has broken your heart? I invite you to write it down here.

the wound of loss

When someone or something we love leaves or is taken away from us, our hearts break.

Since your loss, maybe you've felt as if your heart has been torn down the middle. That's what loss often feels like. A wrenching, ragged tear. A gaping wound.

IT HURTS. IT THROBS. IT ACHES. IT BLEEDS.

In a very real sense, you've been wounded by loss.

You have sustained an injury. But—and this is also important!—you are not ill. Grief is not a disease or sickness. It is also not a disorder. There is nothing intrinsically "wrong" with you. Instead, something from the outside has impacted you.

You are wounded, not ill. You are injured, not sick. You are broken, not diseased.

A note on ambivalence

Here at the outset, let's also agree that **our hearts can be both broken and happy at the same time.**

Some losses are simultaneously gains. For example, a divorce may be both a heartbreaking loss and a hopeful fresh start.

And sometimes a significant loss occurs alongside a profound joy, such as when a family experiences the death of an elder and the birth of a baby in the same month.

The word "ambivalence" means to feel two opposing ways at the same time. If you are ambivalent right now, if your heart is both grief-stricken and glad, this book is also for you.

First aid for broken hearts

OK, so you've been seriously wounded. Now what?

Now you need first aid. Now you need immediate, practical, hands-on care.

Let's say you fall from a ladder and break your arm. You hear the sickening crunch. You feel the excruciating pain. You see that your arm now bends the wrong way.

What do you do?

Do you ignore the injury and continue on with your day and your life as best you can? Do you pretend nothing happened?

OF COURSE NOT!

You head to urgent care because it's urgent. Or you rush to the emergency room because it's an emergency.

Yet many people with broken hearts try to ignore their injuries and continue on with their lives as best they can. They don't get immediate care. They don't seek first aid.

It's a mistake that often costs them the fullness of life. **If this book had warning alarms, they would be sounding here.**

But here you are, seeking first aid. **You are not making the mistake of neglecting your wound. You are wise.**

I'm so glad you're here.

Triage

The first step in first aid is *triage*.

> **Tri•age** (pronounced TREE-azh) (*noun*)
> a medical term that means quickly but closely—under bright lights—assessing injuries to determine what's wrong and what needs attention first.

To save a life in the emergency room, first caregivers work to protect the brain, the heart, and the lungs. Only after those systems are treated and safeguarded do they move on to more minor issues.

With broken hearts, triage also means taking a close, honest look at the injury and determining the steps needed to care for it. Those steps will involve self-care as well as care from others. We'll go over them in a bit.

With any kind of injury, the sooner you triage, the better your chance at healing well.

First aid is called first aid because it happens right after an injury.

First aid for broken hearts works the same way.

I hope you've found this book right after your heartbreak. But if you've been carrying around a broken heart for some time, don't despair. Good mending is still possible.

The goal

After a serious physical injury, the steps to wellness are:

1. triage
2. first aid
3. short-term care
4. long-term care
5. healing

In this process, healing the physical injury is the goal.

In this book, it's our shared goal for your emotional and spiritual injury, too.

Essentially, our goal is to get you through the triage, first-aid, and even short-term care steps so that you will be on your **best path to healing**.

This is such a critical goal!

In fact, mending your broken heart may be the most worthy goal you've ever set for yourself. Why?

Because whether you realize it or not, if your broken heart is uncared-for, it can ruin your life.

As a grief counselor,
I've encountered so, so
many people who've chosen
to lock up their broken hearts
and throw away the key.
They mistakenly believe
that if they are "strong and
carry on," they can more
or less ignore their
broken hearts and move
forward anyway.

The trouble is, it doesn't work like that.

When brokenhearted people choose to remain stuck in denial or numbness, they die while they are alive.

People who never give their broken hearts the care and attention they need often go on to experience chronic:

- difficulties with trust and intimacy,
- depression and negative outlook,
- anxiety and panic attacks,
- psychic numbing and disconnection,
- irritability and agitation,
- substance abuse, addictions, and eating disorders,
- and/or physical problems, real or imagined.

And they rarely realize what's happening to them! They might sense that something is off or incomplete, but almost never do they recognize that their ongoing problems are the festering of emotional and spiritual wounds that may have occurred years or decades earlier.

I WANT BETTER FOR YOU. YOU WANT BETTER FOR YOU, TOO, OR YOU WOULDN'T BE HERE.

So let's get mending.

grieve

"MANY OF US SPEND OUR WHOLE LIVES
RUNNING FROM FEELING WITH THE MISTAKEN
BELIEF THAT YOU CANNOT BEAR THE PAIN.
BUT YOU HAVE ALREADY BORNE THE PAIN.
WHAT YOU HAVE NOT YET DONE IS FEEL
ALL YOU ARE BEYOND THAT PAIN."

— KAHLIL GIBRAN

Grief is caused by loss.
And anytime we experience
a significant loss of any kind,
we naturally grieve.

I've already mentioned that my life's calling and privilege is to companion people in grief. And I've already affirmed that your grief is valid and real.

But maybe you aren't feeling comfortable with the word "grief." After all, grief is a word we associate almost exclusively with death. And maybe your heartbreak isn't death-related.

In the Heartbreakers list on page 10, the death of a loved one tops the charts for many people. But what if your loss is one of the others listed? Or what if it's not listed at all?

It's important for you to understand that **death is not the only thing that causes grief.**

And so, if your heart is broken for *any* reason, you are grieving.

You are in grief.

OK, you say. *OK, I'm in grief.*

So...what is grief, anyway?

Good question.

so, what is grief?

Grief is everything you think and feel about the loss during and after the time your heart began to break.

In other words, grief is what goes on inside of you related to the loss.

Grief is the totality of all of your thoughts and feelings about the loss.

Grief is a single-word shorthand for "all of it."

And when you're many things all at once about a loss which is often how it is—that's grief.

When you're sad about
a loss, that's grief.

When you're mad about
a loss, that's grief.

When you're fearful
about a loss, that's grief.

When your body aches
about a loss, that's grief.

Grief and injury

Let's revisit our injury concept here, too.

Your heart has been wounded. And your emotional and spiritual wound has symptoms, just like a physical wound has symptoms.

Remember that imaginary broken-arm injury we talked about earlier? It causes symptoms. One of the symptoms is pain. Your arm hurts. It's probably swollen, which is another symptom. And maybe your head aches from the fall as well. Perhaps you also feel dizzy and weak, as well as other shock symptoms such as nausea and clammy skin.

With physical injuries, we don't really have a specific word that covers all of our symptoms together. We might say we're feeling "crummy" or "terrible," but those are multipurpose adjectives we can use to describe many things.

But with loss, we do have a specific word—a collective noun—that covers all of our symptoms. And that word is "grief." It's a handy term, and it's one I hope you'll come to appreciate.

moody. guilty. overwhelmed. achy. depressed. lonely. mad. hopeless. sad. confused. angry. dizzy. nauseous.

= grief.

How to triage grief

So how do you triage grief?

As we've said, triage means taking a close, honest look at the injury and determining what needs to be done to care for it.

When you break it down, triaging grief involves the following three steps:

1. Acknowledging that you are experiencing grief.

2. Taking stock of and naming the symptoms you are having.

3. Allowing yourself to feel and spend time with the symptoms.

Acknowledging grief

You can't work on mending your broken heart if you're not first acknowledging your grief. I mean really and truly acknowledging it.

1.

This step is the fork in the road where a lot of people veer off into perpetual denial. That's because it's much harder, at least in the moment, to acknowledge loss and grief than it is to deny it or distract ourselves from it.

Here I want to clarify that after a significant loss, *short-term* numbness and denial are normal and even necessary. They protect us from the full force of a reality that is too much to handle all at once.

But after the early hours, days, or weeks have passed and the protective numbness is wearing off, it's time to acknowledge the loss and the grief. And that's where we find ourselves right now.

You acknowledge your grief by admitting to yourself that your heart is broken.

You acknowledge your grief by affirming that your brokenheartedness and its symptoms—in other words, your grief—are important.

You acknowledge your grief by recognizing that working on healing is a priority.

You acknowledge your grief by giving it the time and attention it needs and deserves.

2. Taking Stock of and Naming Symptoms

A few pages from now, I'll be asking you to take stock of and name your grief symptoms. This is a good exercise any time you are feeling your loss.

What you are doing is inventorying your current inner landscape. Instead of trying to distract yourself from your grief, you are turning your attention toward it.

And in turning toward instead of away from your grief, you are being open and honest with yourself. You are allowing your heart to teach you what it needs, and why.

Feeling and spending time with symptoms

With a physical injury, we see pain and distorted bodily reactions as necessary but bad.

The symptoms are necessary because they let us know that something is wrong.

3. The symptoms are bad because they're not normal and they often hurt.

With a physical injury, typically our goal is to stop the symptoms ASAP and return to normal as soon as possible.

OK, that makes sense.

With an emotional injury, it's also common in our culture to see our symptoms as necessary but bad.

Knowingly or unknowingly, we often believe that our grief may be necessary, or at least unavoidable. And we believe that our painful thoughts and feelings—like the discomfort, swelling, nausea, and other symptoms caused by the broken arm—should be gotten rid of as quickly as possible.

But I'm here to tell
you that this thinking is
wrongheaded.

When we are brokenhearted,
grief is necessary and good.

"Emotional pain is good?," you ask. *"C'mon."*

Yes. After a loss, grief is not only unavoidable, it's *helpful*. It's helpful because it's functional. It serves a purpose. It forces us to slow down, remember, and ponder.

Grief takes time

Turning inward, remembering, and pondering are necessary steps in mending broken hearts.

They are part of the triage stage of grief.

In medicine, effective triage happens quickly.

In the emergency room, it would take just minutes for our broken arm to be examined, X-rayed, assessed, and diagnosed.

In grief, on the other hand, triage happens rather slowly.

We'll soon be triaging your grief as you are experiencing it today, but that will only help you acknowledge, take stock of, and feel *today's* grief. It will help you slow down, remember, and ponder *today*.

Tomorrow will be a new day, and you will still be grieving. You will need to triage, slow down, remember, and ponder again. This will go on for some time.

In grief, triage is an ongoing process.

There is no way to instantly mend a broken heart.
But I can promise you this:

If you give your grief the time and attention it deserves in the early weeks and months (or as soon as you read this), the journey will be more meaningful, your day-to-day life will be better, and you will progress to reconciliation of your grief as efficiently and effectively as possible.

preparing to triage

We'll triage your wound next. That means we're going to shine a bright light on your injury as well as the most prominent symptoms it is causing today.

Remember, it's normal to want to look away from a painful wound, but nevertheless we have to muster the courage to examine the injury closely.

I know that triaging your broken heart can feel scary. I understand.

Our culture is terrible at viewing loss as a natural and necessary part of human life. So we teach people to pretend that nothing is wrong. That they're "fine."

We teach people to look away—and even to be ashamed of their losses and their grief. (What we should be ashamed of is how we treat grief and brokenheartedness. Our shared pretense is what's hurting people.)

But right now, looking away is the exact *wrong* thing to do.

I want you to know that when I work with the brokenhearted and we triage their wounds, they almost always find that examining their losses up close is a relief.

Once they start, they feel a heavy weight being lifted.

You can do this. You are so much stronger and more resilient than you realize.

Bcforc we proceed: if you're traumatized

Before we dive in to triaging, though, I want to say one last important thing.

If your heartbreaker has to do with a traumatic event, I urge you to work through your triage with a professional counselor.

Losses due to horrific circumstances such as homicide, suicide, violent accidents, overdoses, natural disasters, abuse, and other disturbing causes often result in a two-part grief.

1. The first part has to do with the specific circumstances of the loss.

2. And the second part has to do with the thoughts and feelings about the consequences of the loss.

I call these two parts together **"traumatic grief."** The first part is commonly referred to as PTSD.

Traumatic events cause a complicated kind of loss injury that usually requires the first-aid skills of a professional therapist.

If this applies to you, I urge you to make an appointment with a trained caregiver then work through the process described in this book with their support.

Please understand that this does not mean you are weak or that something is "wrong" with you. On the contrary, it simply means that your injury may be so severe that—to draw on our medical analogy again—you need the skills and support of an intensive care unit for a period of time rather than simple first aid.

your injury

Now let's take a look at your broken heart.

You're in a safe space, and it's OK to be vulnerable.

In fact, it's essential to be vulnerable. As Brené Brown says, "Vulnerability is the birthplace of innovation, creativity, and change."

So, what happened?

What broke your heart?

It might be one specific loss, or it might be multiple losses that all happened around the same time. OR—and this is also common—it might be an accumulation of significant life losses that is just now really getting to you.

Pretend I am sitting across from you, and tell me the story of how your heart fell in love or grew attached...and then came to be broken.

My heart fell in love/grew attached when

....

....

....

....

....

....

....

....

....

....

....

....

....

My heart broke when

_____

_____

_____

_____

_____

_____

_____

_____

_____

_____

_____

_____

If it feels good to write about your love and heartbreak, I invite you to continue writing on a separate piece of paper or in a blank notebook.

And thank you for sharing. Your story of love and loss is important and precious.

Acknowledging your grief

Say it out loud:

I acknowledge that my heart was broken when (explain)...

I acknowledge that my grief is important.

I acknowledge that I need to work on my healing.

I acknowledge that my grief needs my time and attention.

In acknowledging your broken heart and your grief, you've taken a significant first step toward mending it.

Taking Stock of Your Symptoms

Now let's triage your symptoms of brokenheartedness.

For now we'll stick to the thoughts and feelings inside you—in other words, your grief. Outward behaviors and actions can be symptoms of your grief, too, and we'll talk about those in Part 2 of this book.

Like most people, you've probably experienced lots of different grief symptoms since the moment your heart began to break.

Grief is like that. It's composed of a wide range of thoughts and feelings. And it tends to shift, change, and circle back on itself from day to day, week to week, and month to month.

I've made a list of the most common grief symptoms that people share with me. Please circle those you have encountered since your loss, then put a star next to any you are feeling most strongly today.

If any of your symptoms aren't on the list, please add them in the spot marked "other."

common grief feelings

Since my loss, I've felt...

Abandoned	Disorganized
Afraid	Distraught
Angry	Embarrassed
Anxious	Empty
Ashamed	Encouraged
Betrayed	Envious
Bewildered	Fearful
Bitter	Fed up
Blameful	Flustered
Confused	Fragmented
Crazy	Frantic
Crushed	Frightened
Defeated	Frustrated
Depressed	Furious
Desolate	Guilty
Desperate	Happy
Devastated	Hateful
Disbelieving	Helpless
Disgusted	Hopeless

Horrified

Hurt

Irritable

Jealous

Joyful

Judgmental

Lonely

Lost

Loveless

Mad

Numb

OK

Overwhelmed

Panicked

Powerless

Rageful

Regretful

Relieved

Resentful

Sad

Scared

Shocked

Stunned

Surprised

Terrified

Terrorized

Trapped

Unwanted

Weak

Worried

Worthless

Yearnful

Zoned out

Physical symptoms:

....

....

....

....

Other:

....

....

....

....

Feeling and spending time with your symptoms

Now that you've acknowledged and named your grief symptoms, it's time to spend some time with them.

This is often the hardest part of grief work. (And yes, grief *is* work.)

We don't like to experience painful thoughts and feelings. And our culture often teaches us that we shouldn't *have* to experience painful thoughts and feelings. (And if we really must experience them, we should do it somewhere behind closed doors, where no one else has to witness our pain.)

So we're usually pretty good at ignoring or distracting ourselves from our painful thoughts and feelings.

But as I said before, our grief thoughts and feelings are *functional*.

They're there for a reason.

But to learn what they have to teach us, we have to feel them and spend time with them.

So now we're going to slow down, remember, and ponder.

First, pick one of the feelings you starred on pages 44-45. It's a feeling you're feeling really strongly today.

You've identified the feeling. You've named the feeling.

Now you're turning inward even further, to really feel the feeling.

Where and how do you feel the feeling in your body? Can you describe the physical sensation?

What thoughts are you having that you associate
with this feeling?

What memories do you have that you associate
with the loss and this feeling?

Next, sit with this feeling for a while. Feel it in your body. Think it with your thoughts. Experience it with your memories.

Try to place your awareness on nothing but this feeling for **at least five to ten minutes.**

I know this practice is challenging, but over time, it will help you mend.

When you're done, let's talk some more.

OK, how did that go?

Did your experience of the feeling change at all from the beginning of the immersion session to the end of the session? If so, how?

How do you feel now?

In my experience companioning thousands of grieving people, **grief usually gets harder before it gets easier.** So especially if your loss is relatively recent, that's something to keep in mind. I don't tell you this to depress or scare you but instead to help you adjust your expectations.

It's also important to remember that **with grief, there is no quick fix.** Grief is a one-day-at-a-time journey.

But this process of acknowledging and befriending feelings—of turning inward, remembering, and pondering—is what helps you begin to reconcile yourself to these feelings.

It's true—you have to feel it to heal it.

Instead of ignoring or fighting these feelings, you embrace them as you would a hurting child. You empathize with them. You appropriately wallow with them when they are crying out to be heard.

And every day that you make the time and muster the courage to turn inward, remember, and ponder, you're moving one step closer to healing.

Fostering hope

We've said that triaging grief involves acknowledging your grief, taking stock of and naming your symptoms, and spending time with those symptoms.

But there's really a fourth component—a special ingredient, if you will. And before we move on to Part 2, we need to remind ourselves that it's a vital part of our first-aid kit.

Human life is full of heartbreak. As I write this, another school shooting has just taken place minutes from my home. Yesterday it was announced that a million species of life on earth may become extinct within decades.

Human heartbreak is all around us. Then there is our own personal heartbreak—so close and so devastating.

But still, we can choose to have hope.

Life may be change and heartbreak, but it is also joy, love, and meaning.

It is all of that.

So, what is hope? Hope is an expectation of a good that is yet to be.

If we believe that our futures can include sparks of joy, love, and meaning, we have hope.

Even as we are spending time with our grief, we can and must also spend time with our hope.

this grief<—>hope
back-and-forth is a seesaw,
and we need to find a
balance that works for us.

We can foster hope in any number of ways:

- spending time with people and pets who love us
- doing activities we care about
- spending time in nature
- engaging in spiritual practices
- planning future activities that excite us
- relishing daily treats
- helping others
- taking care of our bodies, minds, and souls

First aid for broken hearts is about acknowledging and grieving, yes, but it's also about hoping.

That's why you seek out first aid, right?

Because you believe you can get better.

And that, in a nutshell, is hope.

You have it. I have it. Let's carry it with us into Part 2: Mourn.

PART 2

Mourn

"ANYTHING THAT'S HUMAN IS MENTIONABLE,
AND ANYTHING THAT IS MENTIONABLE CAN BE MORE
MANAGEABLE. WHEN WE CAN TALK ABOUT OUR
FEELINGS, THEY BECOME LESS OVERWHELMING,
LESS UPSETTING, AND LESS SCARY. THE PEOPLE
WE TRUST WITH THAT IMPORTANT TALK CAN HELP
US KNOW THAT WE ARE NOT ALONE."

— FRED ROGERS

what is mourning?

Mourning is the secret sauce of grief.

Mourning, not so much the mere passage of time, is what mends broken hearts.

I often say that grief waits on welcome, not on time.

Mourning is the welcome.

Time can help, but only if triage and active mourning are also underway.

If grief is the triage stage of brokenheartedness, mourning is the treatment.

grief in motion

Grief is what goes on inside you when your heart is broken.

Mourning is what goes on outside you when you express your grief.

Grief is internal.

Mourning is external.

Grief is feeling, thinking, turning inward, remembering, and pondering.

Mourning is talking, acting, doing, creating, and moving.

Mourning is grief in motion.

And it's the motion that creates momentum and change.

We've said that in human life, change in the external circumstances of our lives is constant and inevitable. When I say that mourning creates change, I'm talking about internal, emotional change.

To change our internal heartbreak into healing and growth, we must not only pay attention to it internally, we must also express and share it externally.

We must *do* something with our grief.

We must mourn.

mourning is natural

We're born knowing how to mourn.

From the moment we take our first breaths, we respond to distress by crying.

Crying is a natural form of mourning.

When we are distressed infants, we also tip our heads back and jerk our arms and leg. As we grow into toddlerhood, we learn to stomp, shove, and cling to others when we are upset.

And soon we begin to speak and wail our grief. When we're small children, we tell others about every little loss. We express our grief in both bodily behaviors and words.

In short, **we're built to mourn**. But then our culture typically takes our normal and necessary expression of loss away from us.

Hurdles to mourning

We've said that our culture is bad at grief. It promotes the idea that loss is often shameful. And even when it's not shameful, it's something we shouldn't burden other people with.

Instead, we are usually taught, we just have to suck it up, get over it, and move on.

We have it so, so wrong.

If our culture doesn't do grief, it *really* **doesn't do mourning**.

And so, some people will be uncomfortable when you cry, vent, or talk about your heartbreak.

That's OK. There are others who will understand that feeling and expressing emotions is healthy. Those are the people you will seek out right now. Those are the people you will entrust with your "important talk," as Mr. Rogers called it.

And you *yourself* might be uncomfortable mourning. Through no fault of your own, you might be contaminated by our cultural backwardness about loss and grief.

That's OK. You can learn to mourn. Mourning is a learnable skill. This book will help you.

Holistic mourning

In medicine we have holistic treatment. It might involve traditional medical care such as surgery and pharmaceuticals but also includes complementary therapies such as massage therapy, acupuncture, Reiki, biofeedback, and more. The idea is to treat the whole person and not just the physical injury.

In mourning we also need to think holistically.

If we do our grief work but we're not taking care of our bodies, we can't fully heal.

If we do our grief work but withdraw from friends and families without later rebuilding those relationships, we can't fully heal.

Our brokenheartedness affects us physically, cognitively, emotionally, socially, and spiritually.

Our treatment plan—our mourning—needs to address all of these aspects of our selves as well.

to mend our broken hearts,
we must intentionally
seek out ways to express
our grief as we care for
ourselves physically,
cognitively, emotionally,
socially, and spiritually.

How to mourn

You've triaged your grief today. You've spent time feeling, thinking, turning inward, remembering, and pondering.

Now I want you to build mourning into your day as well.

Remember, mourning is grief expressed outside of yourself in some way.

Crying is mourning. If you feel like crying, please, cry. Human tears from grief release stress chemicals. They also alert others to the truth that you are hurting and need and deserve support.

These are all mourning

Talking to friends or family (or a pet!) about your heartbreak. My precious pup Zoey has been an excellent grief therapist for me.

Talking out loud to yourself about your heartbreak

Telling people your story of love and loss

Participating in a support group (formal or informal)

Sharing your heartbreak with a therapist

Journaling. Writing down your thoughts and feelings is a form of outward expression.

Prayer and meditation. They are both ways of trying to connect with something outside of you, something greater than your earthbound reality.

Yelling, pacing, creating art, and sorting through mementos. Doing something with your body that expresses your grief in any way is mourning.

Taking part in spiritual activities.

Volunteering/helping others is ways related to your loss.

Participating in rituals (more on that in a minute).

Just as there may be multiple ways to treat a physical wound, there are lots of ways to mourn.

Grab a pencil and skim through page 63 again. Circle any mourning activities that you are already doing or that seem like the best fit for you moving forward. Then write down any others you can think of here:

There. Now you have a mourning to-do list.

Triage, then treat.

Grieve, then mourn.

Mourn, then mend.

Mend, then thrive.

The role of other people in your mourning

We humans are social creatures.

And our emotional expressions have social functions.

When we're born, we cry to let other people know we need to be taken care of.

When we're heartbroken, we cry and express our grief outside of ourselves in part to let other people know we need to be taken care of.

The empathy, support, love, and companionship of others is essential to our healing when we're brokenhearted.

This works in two main ways.

Relationships with other people help us heal indirectly by giving us something to live for.

One main premise of this book is that our loves and attachments are what give our lives meaning.

1.

So when we're brokenhearted, even though a significant love or attachment has been severed in some way, we still have other loves and attachments that can keep us afloat.

It's like we're on a raft in that winding river of life we talked about. The raft is made up of our relationships, loves, and attachments. The raft holds us up and keeps us safe no matter how scary the river gets.

And when a piece of the raft breaks off because of a loss, we still have a raft to cling to.

The remaining people, loves, and attachments in our lives are your life raft right now. They are the foundation upon which your healing will take place and new loves and attachments can be added.

As you grieve and mourn in ways that work for you, the people who care about you are there to hold you up and give you something to live for.

other people can help us heal directly by giving us empathy and support.

People listen to each other's troubles.

They talk to each other about what's going on in their lives—and their hearts—and they use their natural empathy and caring to help each other feel supported and loved.

As you work to mend your broken heart, your remaining relationships that give you indirect support are your life raft. But the direct help of others is a lifejacket.

No matter how battered and torn apart your raft gets, a lifejacket will keep your head above water.

You need and deserve this kind of one-on-one, focused understanding right now. You need people who can listen without judgment or advice-giving and who can empathize with your heartbreak.

Not everyone can be a lifejacket, however.

In my experience, about a third of the people in your life are neutral when it comes to grief support. They neither help you nor hinder you.

Another third are harmful. They are toxic to the grief healing process, so it is best to cut them loose from the raft altogether.

But the final third are helpful. They are your lifejackets. Tell them you need to talk, and what you hope is they'll listen and empathize without judgment or advice-giving.

And you don't need an entourage. The kind listening ears of even one other person can make all the difference.

But what if you want to keep your grief private?

I understand that heartbreak often feels like an intensely private matter.

The causes of your heartbreak might be complicated and intimate.

You might feel that since no one else experienced the precise attachment and love you experienced, no else can really and truly understand your grief.

And you might be a naturally introverted person— someone who processes things with a great deal of thought and recharges best by being alone.

But even if all of this is true for you, it's still essential to share your heartbreak with at least one other person.

Shhhhh.

If you don't, you're keeping it a secret.

If you don't, you're bottling it up inside you.

If you don't, you're not being true to your most heartfelt pain, hopes, and dreams.

So take the risk of sharing your story with at least one caring listener on an ongoing basis. Your courage will be rewarded a hundredfold.

The role of rituals in your mourning

I said that mourning is the secret sauce of grief.

It's true, but I have another, even secreter insider tip for you:

→ **Rituals are the secret sauce of mourning.**

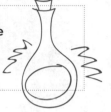

It took me a while to figure this out.

Over my decades as a grief counselor and educator, I began to notice that some broken hearts mended more quickly—even among people who had suffered truly profound and traumatic losses.

Slowly I discerned that many of these super-healers had something in common.

They triaged and mourned their grief—yes.

They searched for spiritual meaning—yes.

They often had good support from friends and family—yes.

But there was also something else—something unassuming and rather simple—that seemed to lift them up and carry them on a current of hope. What was it?

often unknowingly,
these grievers had
leveraged the power
of ritual to supercharge
their healing.

They participated in and often created small,
everyday rituals that helped them both
grieve and mourn their losses.

They did things like this:

- They meditated on a loss-related intention, such as to be as kind and generous as their loved one who had died.

- They journaled their gratitude regularly.

- They walked in nature while purposefully thinking about their love and loss.

- If the loss was related to a love they wanted to continue to cherish, they gathered small objects that symbolized their story of love and loss, and they spent time each day holding and contemplating these symbols. They perhaps carried one of the symbols in their pocket at all times, or they wore it on a chain around their neck.

- If the loss was related to an attachment that was ending (such as a divorce or break-up), they gathered up objects that represented this former attachment and said goodbye to them when they were ready. They performed various rituals of leave-taking that helped integrate the loss into their lives.

- They set aside a few minutes each day to set an intention, light a candle, feel their feelings, and affirm hope.

If you want to supercharge your healing, I highly recommend mourning rituals. Your rituals can be anything that feels calming, healing, and hopeful to you.

Rituals often include some combination of intentionality, actions, symbolism, sequence, presence, heart, and spirit.

Add little rituals to your mourning treatment plan and supercharge your healing.

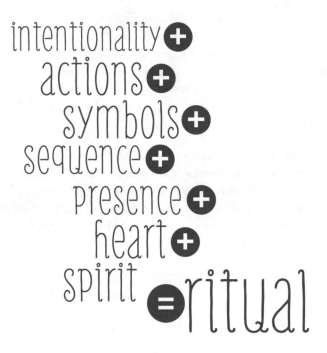

intentionality+
actions+
symbols+
sequence+
presence+
heart+
spirit =ritual

And what if you choose not to mourn?

For some people, mourning is scary.

Expressing grief over and over again
may sound too painful.

Sharing intimate thoughts and feelings with others
may feel too vulnerable and out of control.

And so, at this point, some of you may reason,
"I'll just triage my grief and give it some
attention inside myself. That's hard enough.
That will be enough."

But as a witness to grievers for decades,
one thing I know is this:

UNMOURNED
GRIEF IS
GRIEF THAT
DOESN'T
SOFTEN
OR CHANGE.

When you carry grief inside of you and don't give it all the attention and expression that it needs and deserves, you are setting yourself up for a diminished future—or worse.

On page 23 I talked about getting stuck in denial and numbness. I said that people who don't give their broken hearts all the care they need often go on to experience chronic mental-health, physical, and relationship problems.

I've seen it so many times. It's a sad possibility that I don't want to have happen to you.

Brokenhearted people who move past denial and numbness and work on triaging their grief—turning inward, remembering, and pondering—do get further. They lay the groundwork for the movement that is healing.

But intentional grieving isn't enough.

Intentional mourning is the key that turns the lock.

Grieving without mourning is like triaging without doing anything to treat the injury.

The bottom line: **The action of mourning is essential to mending.**

How to tell if you're done mourning

The bittersweet truth is that wherever love and attachment carry on, grief and mourning carry on as well.

As long as you continue to have feelings of attachment and love for what you lost, you will continue to grieve and mourn. The grief will soften and erupt less often, but it will always be there, stitched into your patchwork heart.

And you will probably have **griefbursts** forever. These are moments of intense grief triggered, often out of the blue, by something that reminds you of the loss.

Yet I believe that to continue to love is to continue to live. Love always gives our lives meaning, even when it's intertwined with grief.

But you picked up this book with hope for healing your broken heart. And that is indeed within your grasp.

Because even though you will almost certainly never completely "get over" your heartbreak and "be done" grieving, it gets better.

It gets so much better.

Fast forward

You came to this resource for first aid. Your heart was raw and deeply wounded, and you needed immediate care.

If you just picked up this book recently, let's fast forward. Let's pretend we're now looking back from the future, perhaps months or a year or two from now.

What has happened?

Well, in the beginning, together we triaged your wound. We shined the light of reality and acknowledgment on it. We took stock of your symptoms and named them. We agreed that you had a significant injury that required attention and treatment.

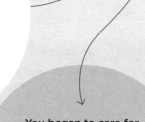

You began to care for your wound by spending time with it, turning inward, remembering, and pondering. This slow, inner-facing process helped you understand and befriend your grief.

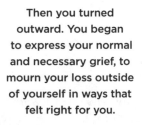

Then you turned outward. You began to express your normal and necessary grief, to mourn your loss outside of yourself in ways that felt right for you.

While you worked on your grief, you cared for yourself physically, cognitively, emotionally, socially, and spiritually as well as you could.

You made healing your broken heart the priority it is, and with intention, you spent time on this healing process almost every day.

And now here you are. You have grown more understanding of your loss. You have made yourself vulnerable, and you have learned vulnerability is worth the risk. You have felt the momentum created by active mourning. You have connected deeply with others. You have experienced sadness and despair but also hope and joy.

And your heart has indeed begun to heal.

your patchwork heart

When a favorite serving bowl cracks and breaks, you might glue it back together. And the repair might hold. Still, the bowl is not as good as new. You can still clearly see the break lines. Little chips might be missing, and the glue itself might be visible in blobs here and there.

But maybe the mended bowl is better than new. It's working again, only now it includes the experience of its life and its loss. It's got character. It's got authenticity. It's got a story to tell.

Your mended heart is the same way. It's a patchwork heart. It's working again, only now it's incorporated its latest experience of loss. It's got character, all right. It's got authenticity. It's got a story to tell. It's been glued back together rather haphazardly, and to some people it might look like a mess.

But it's the joyful, devastating mess that is human life.

You've done the hard work, and now your mended heart is ready to live wholeheartedly again. It's time for Part Three.

PART 3

Live

"A WOUND DOES NOT DESTROY US.
IT ACTIVATES OUR SELF-HEALING POWERS.
THE POINT IS NOT TO 'PUT IT BEHIND YOU'
BUT TO KEEP BENEFITING FROM THE
STRENGTH IT HAS AWAKENED."

— DAVID RICHO

living wholeheartedly

When it comes to first aid for broken hearts, triage is acknowledging, focusing on, and feeling your grief.

Treatment is active mourning.

And then?
And then you live.

When you reach the point that your broken feels tenderly patched and mended, you will be ready to set out on a course to live deeply again.

Mending a broken heart is typically a slow, gradual process instead of a flip of a switch. Over time, you will be able to slowly ease out of active grief and mourning and back into living.

You will continue to grieve and mourn your loss, but the healing-focused activities we've been discussing so far can now start to be replaced by more living-focused activities.

In other words, the balance will shift, with the latter overtaking the former as your broken heart knits back together tighter and tighter.

And if you're intentional about your living—perhaps more intentional than you were before your loss, you won't just zombie-shuffle through the rest of your days. Instead, you will live fully, with meaning and purpose.

you won't just live—you'll thrive.

you will live wholeheartedly.

According to author Brené Brown, living wholeheartedly means living with courage, compassion, and connection.

First, it takes courage.

It takes courage to be vulnerable.

It takes courage to be authentically you.

It takes courage to assert your self-worth.

It takes courage to take risks and reach for what you really, truly want and care about.

And it takes compassion.

It takes compassion to see the good in people.

It takes compassion to forgive yourself and others.

It takes compassion to care for yourself with loving tenderness.

And finally, it takes connection.

It takes active participation in life.

It takes working on and participating in meaningful relationships with other people and the world.

Just as mending your broken heart is an intentional, on-purpose process, so too is living wholeheartedly.

congruence of the heart

Psychologists sometimes talk about the concept of "congruence."

Congruence means that your outer words and behaviors align with your inner feelings.

Congruence means the outside matches the inside.

In other words, if you are congruent, you act and speak in ways consistent with your "gut" as well as your beliefs and values.

For a person who cares about family, for example, congruency would mean she often spends time and attention nurturing togetherness as a family. She would also relate to family members in ways that foster strong relationships.

By grieving and mourning intentionally, you've already been working on congruence. You've been honoring the truth of your internal grief by expressing it on the outside. You've been acknowledging an inner pain by giving it the time, attention, and space it deserves in your life.

Congruence is essential for a simple reason: it makes us feel good. It may not always be easy, but it seems "right." It's truthful and genuine and deeply satisfying.

your mending heart
craves congruence.

Are you listening to it?
Are you learning from it?
Are you living each day
in accordance with
what it truly cherishes?

seeking joy and meaning

Your patchwork heart may want any number of things.

It might want to garden or spend time in nature. It may want to travel. It might want to work toward fulfilling a long-held dream. It may want a kind of companionship and reciprocal love that it doesn't now have.

In my experience, patchwork hearts are wiser than hearts that have never been broken. We might even say that **hearts that have suffered great loss and done the hard work of grieving and mourning are rewarded with wisdom**. They're rewarded with the opportunity to live on with a much better understanding of what matters.

Have you felt this happening to you?

What may once have been important to you may now seem trivial. And what is truly important in your heart of hearts may now take on the clarity of glass.

I find that if they weren't already before their significant loss, the healing-hearted begin to instinctively seek two things: joy and meaning.

Joy is experienced through intentional appreciation of the many pleasures—big and small—of human life on earth.

And meaning? Meaning is found in congruency, which we just talked about.

(Not everything that's joyful is meaningful, and not everything that's meaningful is joyful. But sometimes, happily, they do overlap.)

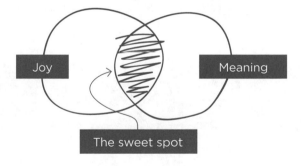

Joy

Meaning

The sweet spot

So how do you find joy and meaning? You can start to build more joy and meaning into your days by living mindfully.

living mindfully

To me, living mindfully is about training our awareness to give attention to our divine sparks—that flicker of light inside of us that tells us what we care about and even feel passionate about.

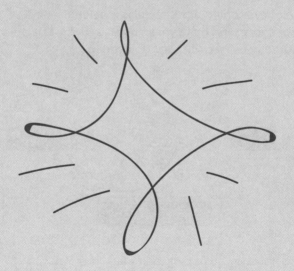

Our awareness then becomes a tool for interacting with the world in ways that feed our souls.

Mindfulness is about enjoying life and making the most of it in the moment, as it unfolds. It's about relishing our precious time on earth. This is the seeking joy part.

But it's *also* about using our discerning awareness each day to make meaningful choices whenever there's a fork in the road.

Joy and meaning.
Meaning and joy.

When all is said and done, life on earth is a marvelous opportunity. It's a smorgasbord of delights, and it presents all of us with possibilities to build loving relationships and meaningful accomplishments.

It's replete with joy and, yes, heartbreak.

Yet whether we truly experience all of that—the delights, the relationships, the accomplishments, the joy, the heartbreak—depends on our willingness and dedication to intentional, mindful living, one day at a time.

paying attention to wonder and beauty.

feeling worthy of and grabbing
hold of joy.

cultivating gratitude.

living on purpose.

living with intention.

living congruently.

pursuing congruent dreams and
meaningful goals.

living more fully than you ever
have before.

The amazing thing is that your patchwork heart *wants*
to live mindfully. It craves wonder, joy, gratitude, and
congruence.

The ironic thing is that to live mindfully, it's your *mind*
that will likely need some training.

stepping outside your mind

As I said, your patchwork heart is wise. It's where your divine spark lives. It's the seat of your soul.

Your mind, on the other hand, may be unwise. It's where your fear and any feelings of unworthiness, envy, judgment, and hate live. It's the seat of your ego.

The funny thing is, most of us were taught the reverse. We were taught our minds are wise and our hearts are fickle—but actually, that's backward.

Unlearning to listen to your mind and instead pay attention to your heart will likely take practice. Mindfulness techniques like meditation and focused presence will help you begin to ignore the tyranny of your mind.

We talked about congruence and deeply held beliefs and values. Sometimes some of our deeply held beliefs and values are false because they are the products of our ego-minds and not our hearts.

Fortunately, your newly emboldened patchwork heart can help you discern the difference.

EGO OR HEART?

Here's a litmus test:

If a belief or value you hold is based on judgment or fear (fear of not having or being enough—which often feels like the need to have more or be more—or judgment or fear of others), it's probably ego-mind-created.

If a belief or value you hold is based on empathy and love (love of self, empathy for others, connection to others, service to others, love of life), on the other hand, it's probably heart-created.

The heart-created stuff is the real stuff.

Finding meaning again

Grieving people often tell me that they struggle to find a reason to get out of bed in the morning.

It's true that in the midst of heartbreak, life can seem utterly devoid of meaning. Worse, it can feel like heartbreak itself is the only meaning of life. And who wants to live in a world where that is the case?

If you're reading this and you're still in the triage stage of first aid, I urge you to hold fiercely to the belief that it can and will get better. Because it will.

The process of triage is actually the beginning and foundation of finding meaning again.

And the process of treatment through active and intentional mourning is where momentum toward meaning really begins to build.

I would say there are two levels of finding meaning again.

One is that basic level of finding a reason to get out of bed on any given day. The reason might be something small. It might be because you're having lunch with someone you care about. Or it might be because a coworker needs your help with a project. Or maybe it's because you have a pet that needs feeding or a loved one who needs your presence or bills that need paying.

In the triage and early treatment phases, finding these little reasons to get out of bed on any given day may be meaning enough.

But as your broken heart begins to mend and you achieve more healing momentum through mourning, you'll be ready to reach for higher meaning.

If you're ready, your patchwork heart is probably telling you where this higher meaning lies.

So what does your heart want?

Does it want a close relationship it doesn't now have? Does it yearn for a career path that feels meaningful? Does it seek adventure? Does it want to fulfill a dream? Is it tugging at you to serve others or a cause in some way?

If you're ready to explore this second level of meaning, let's find out. Let's ask your heart what it wants.

Here are a few questions that might help give it voice.

What have been the most meaningful parts of your life so far?

When you hope or daydream, what do you imagine for your future life?

If you suddenly found out you were going to die in a week, what are the main things that you would regret not having done in life?

If you could wave a wand and have anything you wanted that didn't cost a lot of money, what would that look like?

OK, if you've answered these questions, you've probably jotted down a number of possible connections that your patchwork heart finds meaningful. Now write the ones that feel most important to you in list form here:

....

....

....

....

....

....

....

....

....

....

Next put a question mark to any that seem like they might be mind- or ego-created, and circle any that feel the most truly, deep-down, meaningfully heartfelt to you.

To find higher-level meaning, you'll need to actively, intentionally pursue the items you've circled.

You'll need to set goals and take baby steps one day at a time toward them.

I know you can do it because if you're following the treatment plan, you're mourning and living intentionally each day already.

But most of all I know you can do it because you have a superpower.

Your superpower is the same thing that brought you to this book.

Your superpower is your patchwork heart.

It may not look pretty or feel powerful to you right now, but I assure you, it's the source of all your future joy and meaning.

And even though it's been shattered and it's being glued haphazardly back together, it's much stronger and wiser than it was before.

Risking love and attachment again

I said it before and I'll say it again:

If we're lucky, we love. If we're fortunate, we become attached.

Our loves and attachments are what give our lives meaning and joy.

Which means that no matter which items you circled on page 102, love and attachment will be involved.

And mustering the courage and intention to take that risk again is everything.

Because the alternative is building a wall around your patchwork heart. And a walled-in heart lives an empty and lonely existence, no matter how much you try to delude yourself otherwise.

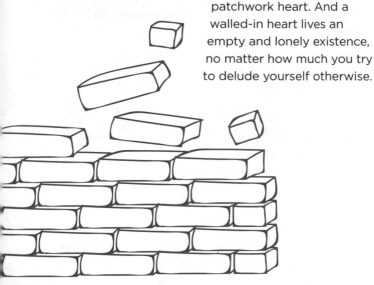

Of course, you may or may not choose to pursue the *same type* of love or attachment that caused your heartbreak.

If your spouse or partner died, for example, I'm not saying that you must find a new spouse or partner to rebuild a meaningful life.

If your heart wants that kind of close relationship again, intentionally seeking it might be right for you. It's right for many people.

But if your heart is telling you it's not interested in (or ready for) another spouse or partner, that's of course a perfectly legitimate choice as well.

You can never really replace an attachment or love that broke your heart anyway. You can only work on building new attachments and loves.

What's important is not so much the relationship labels you choose to pursue but rather building close enough attachments and loves in your life that your patchwork heart feels deep meaning and satisfaction again.

Contentedness is a good indicator. Not complacency— which means accepting just OK or blah instead of good—but true contentment. True contentment is rich in gratitude and, on its best days, brimming with joy.

True contentment is the kind of a day-to-day deep satisfaction that only comes from an imperfectly perfect life, well and truly lived.

what if your heart breaks again?

It will.

If you are fortunate to continue to live on
for a while, your heart will almost
certainly be broken again.

Life is change, remember?

The globe spins. The years pass.
And things change.

people get sick.

people age.

people die.

pets too.

people betray us.

we betray ourselves.

passions ebb and flow.

fortunes rise and fall.

the river of life takes us around an unexpected or too-soon bend...and once again we find that our patchwork hearts explode into a pile *of rubble.*

But the next time your heart breaks, you will be better prepared.

You will know how to triage your wound.

You will know how to treat your wound.

And you will know how to create momentum toward a renewed life of meaning and purpose again.

It will still hurt. A lot. Knowing what to do with the hurt doesn't prevent the hurt.

But it does make the hurt more of a—dare I say it?—friend.

If you've befriended your pain over your current heartbreak, you've learned that it's not your enemy. Instead, it's your love in a different form. And love is always good.

Yes, if you live long enough, your heart will almost certainly break again. That is, if you're lucky. If you're lucky enough to have built and nurtured more strong loves and attachments.

So here's to love and attachment. And here's to heartbreak.

A continued life of grace

Here we are in this mindboggling time in human history
on this staggeringly beautiful planet in
this unfathomable universe together.

Aren't we lucky?

I believe we've been blessed by grace.

Grace is the divine mechanism by
which anything good we've received
in life has been given to us.

Grace gave us life.

Grace gave us love.

Grace generously bestowed on us every gift
we've ever been given.

After all, we didn't *earn* life. And we don't always *deserve*
the love we receive.

We're the beneficiaries of good old grace in action.

**Intentionally cultivating gratitude for this grace, for this
life, is key to living forward with joy and meaning**.

And this life is full of heartbreak. Both beautiful and
terrible things happen every day. They certainly have in
my life. What about yours?

So to be grateful for this life is to be grateful for...*all of it*.

Albert Einstein famously said,

"THERE ARE ONLY TWO WAYS TO LIVE YOUR LIFE. ONE IS AS THOUGH NOTHING IS A MIRACLE. THE OTHER IS AS THOUGH EVERYTHING IS A MIRACLE."

I choose the latter. I hope you will too.

A Final word

"BE IN LOVE WITH YOUR LIFE. EVERY MINUTE OF IT."

— JACK KEROUAC

As I live out my calling as a caregiver, I hear about heartbreak every day. I consider myself privileged to be a confidant for grievers and grief caregivers across the globe. They tell me their stories of love, attachment, and loss. I listen, and I learn.

Imagine me as I travel each month to speak and teach. Everywhere I go, people bring me their grief.

I witness a lot of pain, it's true, but here's the thing: I witness even more love and hope.

As you struggle with your own heartbreak, it might help you to know that you're not alone. So many others out there share your experience.

In this little book I've boiled down the lessons all these many thousands of grievers have taught me.

They want you to know:

You can muster the courage to triage your grief.

You can find the strength to treat yourself with active and honest mourning.

you can heal and go on to truly live life with meaning and purpose.

I am not the expert—they are. I am just the humble bearer of their good tidings.

Thank you for entrusting me with your broken heart. It's the most tender, precious thing in all the world.

Be gentle with it. Be kind to it.

Listen to its whispers.

Act on its passions.

Carry out its yearnings.

Heed its wisdom.

Patch it together and make it whole again.

And whenever you're struggling and need a quick refresher, just pick up this book and give it a skim.

You know what to do.

godspeed.

About the author

Alan D. Wolfelt, Ph.D. is a respected author and educator on the topics of companioning others and healing in grief. He serves as Director of the Center for Loss and Life Transition and is on the faculty at the University of Colorado Medical School's Department of Family Medicine. Dr. Wolfelt has written many bestselling books on

healing in grief, including *Understanding Your Grief*, *Healing Your Grieving Heart*, and *The Mourner's Book of Hope*. Visit www.centerforloss.com to learn more about grief and loss and to order Dr. Wolfelt's books.

Also by Alan Wolfelt

Loving from the Outside In, Mourning from the Inside Out

"The capacity to love requires the necessity to mourn," writes Dr. Wolfelt in this lovely new gift book. "In other words, love and grief are two sides of the same precious coin. One does not—and cannot—exist without the other. They are the yin and yang of our lives. What higher purpose is there in life but to give and receive love? Love is the essence of a life of abundance and joy. No matter what life brings our way, love is our highest goal, our most passionate quest. People sometimes say that grief is the price we pay for the joy of having loved. If we allow ourselves the grace that comes with love, we must allow ourselves the grace that is required to mourn."

In this compassionate guide, Dr. Wolfelt explores what love and grief have in common and invites the reader to mourn well in order to go on to live and love well again.

ISBN: 978-1-61722-147-7 • Price: $15.95 • 96 pages

All Dr. Wolfelt's publications can be ordered by mail from:
Companion Press, 3735 Broken Bow Road, Fort Collins, CO 80526
(970) 226-6050 • www.centerforloss.com

Also by Alan Wolfelt

The Journey Through Grief
Reflections on Healing
SECOND EDITION

This revised, second edition of
The Journey Through Grief takes
Dr. Wolfelt's popular book of
reflections and adds space for
guided journaling, asking readers
thoughtful questions about their
unique mourning needs and
providing room to write responses.

The Journey Through Grief is organized around the six
needs that all mourners must yield to—indeed embrace—
if they are to go on to find continued meaning in life and
living. Following a short explanation of each mourning
need is a series of brief, spiritual passages that, when
read slowly and reflectively, help mourners work through
their unique thoughts and feelings.

ISBN 978-1-879651-11-1 • 152 pages • hardcover • $21.95

All Dr. Wolfelt's publications can be ordered by mail from:
Companion Press, 3735 Broken Bow Road, Fort Collins, CO 80526
(970) 226-6050 • www.centerforloss.com

Also by Alan Wolfelt

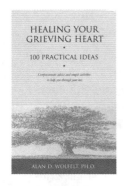

Healing Your Grieving Heart
100 Practical Ideas

When someone loved dies, we must express our grief if we are to heal. In other words, we must mourn. But knowing what to do with your grief and how to mourn doesn't always come naturally in our mourning-avoiding culture.

This book offers 100 practical ideas to help you practice self-compassion. Some of the ideas teach you the principles of grief and mourning. The remainder offer practical, action-oriented tips for embracing your grief. Each also suggests a carpe diem, which will help you seize the day by helping you move toward healing today.

ISBN 978-1-879651-25-8 • 128 pages • softcover • $11.95

All Dr. Wolfelt's publications can be ordered by mail from:
Companion Press, 3735 Broken Bow Road, Fort Collins, CO 80526
(970) 226-6050 • www.centerforloss.com

Also by Alan Wolfelt

Grief One Day at a Time
365 Meditations to Help You Heal After Loss

After someone you love dies, each day can be a struggle. But each day, you can also find comfort and understanding in this daily companion. With one brief entry for every day of the calendar year, this little book offers small, one-day-at-a-time doses of guidance and healing. Each entry includes an inspiring or soothing quote followed by a short discussion of the day's theme.

How do you get through the loss of a loved one? One day at a time. This compassionate gem of a book will accompany you.

"Each day I look forward to reading a new page...I can't imagine dealing with my sorrow without [this] book."
— A reader

ISBN 978-1-61722-238-2 • 384 pages • softcover • $14.95

All Dr. Wolfelt's publications can be ordered by mail from:
Companion Press, 3735 Broken Bow Road, Fort Collins, CO 80526
(970) 226-6050 • www.centerforloss.com